650 | On Fathers

Edited by Edward McCann

650 | WHERE WRITERS READ

Founder / Editor • Edward McCann
Executive Producer • Richard Kollath
Literary Ombudsman • Steven Lewis
Chief of Operations • Jane Kaupp
Technical Advisor • Conrad Trautmann
Technical Advisor • Stephen Kaupp
Director of Communications • Gretchen Reed
Director of Photography • Kevin O'Connor
Videography/Photography • Adley Atia, Sara Caldwell
Chief Audio Engineer • Jesse Chason
Copy Editor • Kathleen Stanley
Graphic Designer • Diane Fokas
Production Director Emeritus • Gregory Bray

Production Assistants
Christopher Dennison, Diane Fokas, Mackenzie Meeks,
Jackie Mercurio, and Brian Reagher

Editorial Committee
Rachel Aydt, Laura Shaine Cunningham, Angela Davis-Gardner,
Joseph Goodrich, Steven Lewis, David Masello, and Honor Molloy

For all our dads, and all the dads-to-be.

ABOUT 650

"I believe that what we become depends on what our fathers teach us at odd moments, when they aren't trying to teach us. We are formed by little scraps of wisdom."

Those words written by Umberto Eco reflect the experiences of the writers whose work is contained in this volume. They also remind us what many of our fathers (and mothers) told us when we were kids: Actions speak louder than words. The stories on these pages capture some of those actions—and some shared moments that reveal aspects of character that the writers have carried far into their adult lives.

650 is a celebration of writing and the spoken word—a literary forum featuring two-page, 650-word personal stories that can be performed in five minutes. Our events at theaters, colleges, and libraries around the country are organized around single, broad topics that invite a range of expression, and recorded performances are added to a digital archive of writers reading their work aloud. The writers and their work receive additional exposure through podcasts, broadcasts, our YouTube channel, and in these printed volumes. The volume you hold in your hands is a curated collection from a select group of writers featured at our first ever live reading, a sold-out event at The Cell Theater in New York City—an unforgettable show that Malachy McCourt ended by leading the house in a rousing rendition of "Wild Mountain Thyme."

650 features graduate students and grandmothers, first-timers and bestsellers. It's all about the writing, with an emphasis on craft. It's about the choice of one word over another, about the shape of sentences and paragraphs, the arc of a narrative, the poetry of a unique literary voice. If you love language and enjoy a good story, you've come to the right place. To submit your work or attend our shows, visit our website or Facebook page, and join our mailing list. Please tell your friends about us, and **spread the word about the spoken word.**

Ed McCann

Edward McCann, Founder / Editor

READ650.COM
FACEBOOK.COM/READ650

CONTENTS

650 | On Fathers

Edited by Edward McCann

SUZANNE MCCONNELL

Suzanne McConnell holds an MFA in Fiction Writing from the Iowa Writers' Workshop and is Fiction Editor for the Bellevue Literary Revue. Twice nominated for the Pushcart Prize, her writing has appeared in *The Huffington Post, The Hamilton Stone Review, The Saint Ann's Review, Bellevue Literary Review, Calyx, Green Mountains Review, The Fiddlehead, Personal Fiction Writing, Poets & Writers,* HalfthePlanet. com, *Cape Women, Earth's Daughters, A Sense of Place,* and Discovery Channel Publishing's Travel Series. She teaches writing and literature at *Hunter College*. Her most recent book on Kurt Vonnegut's advice on writing, *Vonnegut's Pearls,* will be published as an e-book by Rosetta Books and in hard cover by Seven Stories Press. Suzanne grew up in San Diego and lives in New York City and Wellfleet, Massachusetts, with her husband, sculptor Gary Kuehn.

PAPA: CHRISTMAS 1980

Suzanne McConnell

As usual, you haven't come to meet me at the airport with the others. Yet when we arrive home you rush out from the house. "Susie," you say, and kiss me, unafraid, holding me long around and beneath my shoulders.

So I come to you in the morning. Come out in the cold morning's sweet fog to the memory of hay baled and stacked in the lean-to shack. And you have lost your grim impatience, allow my fumbling bare fingers and short strength to work beside you, loading them on the pickup truck. When it's full, we get inside and begin the drive to the field.

You open the first fence. I offer at the second. "No," you say, "there is a certain way I want to shut it."

"I'll do this one," I say, at the third and last.

You hesitate. "Okay."

You drive the truck through then I climb in again and shut the door back tight.

Out in the field the cows flow to us in a lumbering until they're close around the glass, shouldering. "Better wait to get out," you say, "until after the first bale's thrown. They're pretty feisty."

I'm not afraid of them as I once was; yet, I wait.

1

You draw out your pocketknife to whittle the soft mud from the bottoms of your shoes, bending down in your solitary grace, wiping the blade in sure strokes on the white fence. I watch you, admiring your careful pace, so much slower than my own.

"Now, how 'bout yours," you say. You open your hand and I hold up my foot for you to see. "These cleats sure do get jammed."

"Yes, Papa."

"Here," you say. You take my foot in your hand. I can feel your fingers through my wool sock and around my ankle, over the bone, firmly, gently, and the knife scraping, scraping the mud lodged in the soles.

"There," you say, when it's finished. "You're okay." You set my foot down and we go on into the house with the others.

KENRYA RANKIN

Kenrya Rankin, deputy editor at *Colorlines*, is an award-winning author, journalist, and editorial consultant whose insight has been tapped by leading outlets, including The *New York Times*, The *Huffington Post* and *ThinkProgress*. As a journalist and editor, her work has appeared in national publications, including *Reader's Digest, Ebony, Glamour* and *Fast Company*. She's published three books, including *Bet on Black: African-American Women Celebrate Fatherhood in the Age of Barack Obama,* and is working on a collection for Nation Books called *How We Fight White Supremacy: A Field Guide to Black Resistance*. A native of Cleveland, Ohio and a graduate of both Howard University and New York University, she lives with her daughter in the Washington, DC area.

THE LIGHT

Kenrya Rankin

I'm five. It's dark, cold as our drafty ranch-style house is wont to be, and I can't sleep. As an insomniac from way back, this wasn't unusual. What was odd was the sight that greeted me when I reached the end of the hallway, my bare feet slapping against the freezing tile, tiny hand trailing along the same sharply textured sherbet-colored wall that I'd scraped my arm on when I lost my balance on my Strawberry Shortcake tricycle: Two eyes, looking up and out at me like an old man peering over his reading glasses at an irritation. Then, short eggplant-rinsed hair—my mother, her dark arms akimbo, legs intertwined with a man/some man/not my father.

I told.

My parents eventually separated, then divorced a couple years later. They did a good job of keeping the fallout away from my little sister and me, though I've always felt a bit responsible for their split. But it was bound to happen. It wasn't just the cheating, though I think there was plenty of it. My mother just didn't seem to be cut out for the whole mothering thing. Self-interest often seemed to win out over responsibility, like the day I returned home from morning kindergarten and she wasn't there. I peed in the backyard, careful not to splash my pastel-colored "Wednesday" undies, then rode with Cindy The Bus Driver while she made her afternoon circuit, praying that Mommy would be there when we stopped again. We returned three hours later to find my sister, Leena, on her pink Big Wheel out front, my mother inside.

Daddy got custody on account of his steady job as a computer tech and the top-notch suburban school district where we lived. Even at nine years old, I knew it was a good decision, choosing to bow out of meetings of the Divorced Kids Club that school counselors tried to force me to attend. Courts are reluctant to separate kids from their mothers, but Daddy was doting, tireless, and loving. He was a natural if over solicitous father, staying up all night with an ear to my chest when my asthma threatened to send us down Columbus Road to the ER, running red lights all the way in our blue Ford Taurus station wagon; checking behind doors when I was convinced that Freddy Krueger was going to pirouette out and slash me to pieces, and even playing romantic advisor when I retreated from my unstable on-again-off-again college boyfriend.

But it wasn't always easy. He had to drag Leena and me along on countless late night calls when a mainframe broke down in the over-air conditioned basement of some darkened school. And he struggled with the decision to have me let myself in after class, the first latchkey kid in my group of friends, proudly wearing my two shiny slivers of metal on a woven lanyard around my neck. Then came the day that gig turned out to be not so steady; he and hundreds of others were laid off like so many expendable space monkeys. Subcontracting work followed, but it didn't pay the same way mandatory overtime used to, and we lived without health insurance for years. But he held us together with his trademark earnestness.

I asked Daddy what it was like being a man under pressure

to mold two girls, two ladies. "You always look back and think that you could have done more," was his reply. He wishes he'd been better at communicating with us about all things girly, and regrets that he couldn't give us everything we wanted on his single income. But he was always creative in fatherhood: He subscribed to Essence to keep aspirational black women in our home, even if they were just on our mirrored coffee table. He paid a lady to do our hair every other week so we wouldn't be bully bait. And he kept our older girl cousins around as surrogate moms who accompanied us on back-to-school clothes shopping excursions.

Seeing my daddy in action taught me the greatness that men—fathers—are capable of. And it would be nothing short of self-sabotage to stray away from the pure light that I felt from him, having felt it on my face and soaked it into my spirit.

Reprinted from Bet on Black: African-American Women Celebrate Fatherhood in the Age of Barack Obama (Kifani Press). Learn more about Kenrya Rankin at www.kenrya.com

DAVID MASELLO

David Masello began his career as a nonfiction book editor at Simon and Schuster, then went on to hold senior editorial positions at many magazines, including *Travel & Leisure, Art and Antiques*, and *Town and Country*, where he was features editor. He's currently executive editor of *Milieu*, a magazine about design and architecture. A widely published essayist and poet, his work appears in the *New York Times, Salon, Best American Essays*, and numerous literary and art magazines. His plays have been produced and performed by the Manhattan Repertory Theatre, Jewish Women's Theatre of Los Angeles, Big Apple Theatre Festival, and Fresh Fruit Festival. He is the author of two books about art and architecture. A native of Evanstan, Illinois, he's lived for thirty years in New York City.

SHADOW RUN

David Masello

The first thing my father would say whenever we'd pass the houses in the town of Pass-a-Grille, Florida, is, "I never thought I'd spend so many years of my life living in a place with common walls."

He says this because he has lived in a townhouse development since moving to Florida from Chicago years earlier with his woman-friend of many years, and, now, alone, in a different development. His new locale has the unlikely name of Shadow Run and is situated miles inland from the Gulf and across the road from a missile-components factory. Bored, ornery swans glide over a pond—a muddy ditch fed by a gurgling spigot—their orange bills tracing the still air like embers.

"I'd like to end up in a house," he says as we drive along Gulf Boulevard to Pass-a-Grille.

My father was always a putterer around a house and I know, as we pass these modest dwellings, that he misses the exquisite peace and purpose that comes with the cool grip of a spray gun while seated in a lawn chair, the white, hissing line of water issuing from the nozzle, a prism halo appearing beyond reach. He looks longingly at men his age stooping in yards to retrieve fallen palm fronds.

We always head first to Pass-a-Grille because it is where we both get our bearings during one of my visits. I can acquaint myself there with the unfamiliar blast of heat and sun and he can adjust to suddenly having company and conversation for several days. Despite our excitement at seeing each other, there is a certain shyness, even silence, that results from the months of separation. But the moment we pass the pink-stucco Don Cesar, a glamorous, turreted 1920s hotel that marks the entrance to town, my father sits up in the passenger seat. Our visit has begun.

The road ends at a bunker of sea grass, the tires of my rental car registering sand on the pavement, squalls of it blowing like vaporous ghosts. "I hate that term 'dead end', my father says, pointing to the sign indicating such. "There's got to be a better phrase."

He takes my hand as I hoist him up to the pier fashioned of boulders and as we walk from rock to rock, waves thunk in the crevices strung with spider webs; the occasional stink of rotting fish and seaweed keep us moving. While looking up to a parasailer, a punctuation point like an Icarus, I slip, but catch myself. Instinctively, I turn to catch my father as he, too, falters. We look down to see a thick fold of gray wet blanket on which we had stepped. A dead manta ray—the Spanish word *manta*, for blanket or cape.

After having been in the sun for hours, the creature's grayness was bleaching to a milky opaqueness, its mouth carved like an opening in an ocarina. Strands of seaweed clung to its body like mussed, thinning hair. Neither flies nor pelicans had yet found it. It was still perfect enough to look alive. There was much about its face—a discernible brow, eyes, mouth—to reference a person's, but one that had been distorted, flattened into a saucer by a carnival mirror.

"How the hell did this poor thing get up here," my father says. "You know, it's both repulsive and beautiful. Maybe we ought to throw it back in."

"Why not leave it here," I say.

"Because it seems so—so out of place. Who ever saw one of these things this high up on a rock? Sacrilegious is going a bit far, but it's just not right that it rots like this, alone."

I find a palm branch, sturdy enough to move the fish. Sea lice have gotten to its underbelly, a maggoty mass of them, and I fight a sudden wash of nausea. I move the creature until it falls from the edge, bouncing on a lower breakwater boulder before plopping into the water, tailing beads of air as it sinks. Its wet shadow remains on the rock, already steaming to extinction, but is replaced by another cast by my father and the smoke rising from his pipe.

HONOR MOLLOY

Honor Molloy is the author of the autobiographical novel *Smarty Girl: Dublin Savage*, a fictionalized version of her childhood in Ireland. Her play *Crackskull Row* (*New York Times* Critic's Pick), developed and produced by Nancy Manocherian's the cell, won best production and best direction awards as part of Origin's First Irish Theatre Festival 2016. The Irish Repertory Theatre subsequently moved the cell's production to its W. Scott McLucas Studio Theatre for a seven-week run. An alumna of New Dramatists, Molloy has received support from the National Endowment for the Arts, the New York Foundation for the Arts, and a fellowship year at the Radcliffe Institute for Advanced Study at Harvard. She lives and writes in New York City.

WHAT'S TAKEN

Honor Molloy

My father. Actor. Dubliner. Charmer. Brute. And mystery to me. One time he beat my mother with the intent to destroy the boy growing within—wee Rowan.

And Wee Noleen? She is nowhere. She is enspelled. See, she never left that house on Tolka Row, but wanders the emptied rooms, stays in the hollows of herself, having a big think:

There was a time when tradition held—and tradition held us. When our country held—and our country held us. When our fambilly held—and our fambilly held us. When our home, it held—held together and held us.

Where? Where did that go? That holding.

But mostly, where did it go—the Life *O'Feeney*?

Some time I'll break loose, rejoin the mortal world, she promises her self. But does nothing. And so the years go. The days. The hours. The roarings.

And Noleen stays in that house. Stays small. Never grows. Never goes on to America. Till the one day—*oh murder!*—Pater

13

O'Feeney screeps in. Lurching spavindy. He's seventy years old, he's, blathered and bollixed. Haggard and plunkered, he's bringing his guilt all round. His failure. Drags *that* in through the door to the house he'd built. And then put under.

Da O'Feeney steps into the darkness. The silence in the big downstairs room. The room with no pot oven, no turf, nuthin' but mold oranging the walls. There's a moss-greened carpet of floor 'neath his feet. Black bog dirt pushes wide the cracking cobbles. Time's touching back. A folding of past, the now, the what's-to-come. Day-to-day, one to the other.

What year is it? What year? Two hundert-n-one B.C.—back in the Celtic Age—The Iron?

It's nineteen hundert-n-ninety-the-nine. And him dying. Their da. Returns to Tolka Row. And him dying. Crawls into the dusty fireplace—he curls up. And cries. Cries the bitters.

Oh lament-lament, yuh yellar beggar. His haggers and snorts. His blithering heavings. Divill scorch and scald him for feeling sorry for him selfs. That loather. That Dublin sot—soused all the summers of his life.

Him that trampled his very own son 'til he bled out the hearth. On the Night of Evil Deeds.

And our Rowan won't lie still.

It's Rowan drew back the luck, the love. Drained the pound notes from the fambilly. So their life ran downhill. Rowan's put them to the gutters, his hunger-hunger haunts this house. He's a hungry soul living off Noleen. It's him that whores the splithers of her mind, keeping her here on Tolka Row, trapped with the race of the nightmare. She belongs to the murdered. She drifts 'mong the ghosts of the young.

And Olly cries. On-on he cries. Father of lies. Ould lubber-jester.

And so.

She goes to him. She picks him up. Soothes his blacky hair. Holds him. She rocks him. Holds him. Her father. Her brother. Her son. Her twin. Her mess of a self.

Straddling worlds. The seen. Unseen. The known. Not-known. The understood. Straddling worlds—she loves and loves him. She always will.

He is her crying boy. He is her daddy crying. *Make it stop. O make it stop.*

She can't bear to see this—she
Must pull the sads out of him—she
Takes him then. Takes him. And makes a terrible blunder.

She bends in to his mouth. And Olly locks in. Seizes her jaw so they're kissing. Her father, her father rough-mouths her. Sand grits his tongue. Not saliva, not blood, but sand. He's the smell of cigs. Of bog. He is the whisky jar-man. Too many for her. His sad knocks her breath out. And he sucks her down. Sand snakes her nostrils, ear holes, pores, 'til she peels away from the walls of her self and is suckered down.

She goes inwards and inwards and inwards-further, taking seat in his one lung. She fits there. A caul. His boy? Our Rowan?

No.

She. She is his.

Huddled in.

She is inside him now and holding. Keeping him safe from his self. Safe from his *him.*

'Cause Noleen is certain-sure that she can love him saved.

DAN ZEVIN

Dan Zevin is a Thurber Prize-winning humorist. He has written eight books, including *Dan Gets a Minivan and The Day I Turned Uncool*, which were both optioned by Adam Sandler. Dan has been an award-winning humor columnist for the *New York Times*, a comic commentator for NPR, and a contributor to print or digital editions of *The New Yorker, McSweeney's, Rolling Stone, Salon, the L.A. Times, Real Simple*, and *Parents*, among others. He currently teaches comedic writing at Sarah Lawrence College. Dan's latest project is a series of picture-book parodies featuring adorably annoying adults, including *Mr. Selfie, Little Miss Overshare, Mr. Humblebrag*, and *Little Miss Basic*. Dan lives with his wife, kids, and pet rabbit in the suburbs of New York City, where he has become an active member of his local Costco.

COSTCO

Dan Zevin

"A man should never stop learning, even on his last day," my father tells me. "Maimonides." We're at the entrance to Costco in Union, New Jersey. He's about to demonstrate how to maximize the cargo space of the wide-load shopping carts he has hand-selected for us. "Observe," he says. And with a flick of the wrist, he expands the folding baby seat.

"But why?" I ask. "Why must we expand these baby seats when the kids are at home watching Animal Planet with our wives?"

"All in good time my boy, all in good time. Cervantes."

When the glass doors slide open, I experience a pre-vomit, fight-or-flight sensation. My vision is blurred by an onslaught of flashing, flat-panel screens. A man tries to make me eat free samples of crabmeat salad on a cracker. A guard chases me down, demanding to see my membership card. She notices my father, sorting through his circular.

"Doctor Zevin! I was wondering when you was coming!"

My father knows the bouncer. I can relax.

"I tied her tubes three weeks ago," he tells me, striding by with a smile. As we make our way in, he smiles and waves to several other personnel he seems to know intimately, and most likely does, since he is their gynecologist.

"Follow me," my father says. "Wait'll you see the bananas they got back there. My treat."

Fifteen minutes later, his cart contained the U.S. recommended daily, and yearly, allowance of bananas. He grabbed a bunch—80 or so—and carefully placed them into my cart, along with a mile-long vine of red seedless grapes and the gross national product of Nova Scotia in blueberries.

"To lengthen thy life, lessen thy meals," my father declared. "Benjamin Franklin."

This is how my father talks. In sayings. Walking around Costco with him was like walking around Costco with the author of Bartlett's Familiar Quotations. But Ronald's familiar quotations are way more familiar, at least to his offspring. Over the course of the next few miles, he quoted Gandhi, Einstein, da Vinci, DiMaggio, Jung, and Allen (Woody). The most memorable quote he ever gave me came on my Bar Mitzvah, when he was called to the pulpit to provide fatherly advice. It was from a Rudyard Kipling poem called If. "If you can keep your head when all about you are losing theirs . . . then you'll be a man my son."

Based on that benchmark, I never became a man. But it wasn't until answering my father's clarion call to Costco that I suddenly identified the real roadblock. He was standing in aisle 4,000-B with an ear-to-ear grin and a shrink-wrapped 60-pack of paper towels. Tactfully, he removed himself from the embrace of a supervisor whose nametag read Esther, and upon whom he had recently performed a pap smear. The time had come for him to reveal the secrets of the expandable child seat.

As he instructed, I flipped down the plastic red covering, thus blocking the leg holes. Words were not necessary as he presented me with paper towels. He merely motioned with his chin to put them where the child goes. It was uncanny; a precise fit.

"A new type of thinking is essential if mankind is to survive," my father remarked. "Albert Einstein."

I appreciate my father's generosity, I really do. And I really do wish to emulate his confidence, his level-headedness, his ability to "keep calm and carry on" without the use of anti-anxiety medication.

But something about the paper towel situation made me see what I had to do to be the kind of man my father is. Like Odysseus, son of Laertes, I had to break away. Just like Homer will tell you, it's hard to feel like a man when you're in your forties and your dad is still buying you paper towels.

The next thing I knew, I was on my own--overcome by a powerful, nearly primal pull toward a double-wide flat of Poland Spring mini-bottles. If I wished to replenish my family's water supply, it was up to me now. Seizing my conquest from the shelf, the wisdom of the elder echoed in my mind: "*Use the rack underneath* your shopping cart for oversized flats, Danny. Most people don't even know that's what it's there for."

With the water beneath my cart, I had completed a critical step in my initiation. I was on my way to becoming a provider.

Not long from now, our roles will reverse and I'll be the one providing for him. I'll provide a 76-count case of Depends, a Medline deluxe rolling walker with built-in cup holder, a 30-pack of hearing aid batteries in a choice of orange, brown, or yellow. And, when his time comes, I'll provide him with the one final item we found by the exit doors. It was the Costco coffin. My father quoted Woody Allen as soon as he saw it. "I'm not afraid of death," he said. " I just don't want to be there when it happens." When it does, though, I'm pretty sure I know where he'd like to be buried.

I shall take my son Leo to Costco one day, and Leo shall take his son, and the patriarchal cycle of Zevin providers shall forever continue. In the meantime, I decided to spring for the bananas. Handing my brand new membership ID to the cashier, it struck me that you don't really know what you look like until you've seen your digitized face on the back of a Costco card. On mine, I'm the spitting image of my dad.

CHARLES R. HALE

Charles R. Hale, a descendant of New York Irish famine immigrants, has published a number of ancestral history essays in literary magazines. He's co-founded Artists Without Walls, an organization dedicated to cultural collaboration and artistic achievement. A musical historian and producer, Charles blends imagery and performance art to create uniquely New York experiences. His shows incorporate story, music, imagery, and dance, and include *Crossing Boroughs*, performed at the Museum of the City of New York, *The Musical History of the Lower East Side,* and *New York City: A Shining Mosaic*. His show *Jazz and the City* combines narration with live music—David Raleigh's jazz quartet—in a tribute to the Great American Songbook. The City University of New York has honored Charles for outstanding service to New York and Irish America."

A MAN OF EXTREMES

Charles R. Hale

The Irish poet William Butler Yeats wrote, "Being Irish he had an abiding sense of tragedy, which sustained him through temporary periods of joy."

He must have known my father. One evening he'd be filled with joy . . . I look down from my bedroom window. Here he comes, up the driveway, singing, smoking, whistling, and then, *wham!* His teeth snap down on the filter and the cigarette shoots straight up, just like the old photos I'd seen of Franklin Delano Roosevelt.

"Hi, Dad."

"Hey, c'mon down, Son. Bring your bat and glove."

Yeah.

"A little pepper, Charles?"

Baltimore chops, frozen ropes, balls that paint the black, balls that have seeing eyes, and pepper: Baseball's secret language that only fathers and sons understand. The two of us, lost in the joys of the game, its intricacies, and subsequently, the pleasure of each other's company.

The next evening he'd be filled with sadness . . . I look down from my window. Here he comes, head down, silence. Keep your distance.

With heads lowered, dinner is a rush-job in silence, and then he's off to his corner garden. I watch him from my bedroom window, a cigarette dangling from his lips, his hands thrusting into the soil, digging, always digging, trying to make sense of the obstacles that he'd wrestled with day after day.

On those dark days he'd say nothing.

Nothing.

My father drove me to my first baseball game in his black and white two-tone Buick Roadmaster, the car with the biggest white-wall tires I'd ever seen. He slows the Roadmaster, the moment's sacred, as if I'm being ordained: "There it is," he says, "There it is." And sitting in the front seat with my father, I see it, Brooklyn's temple of worship, Ebbets Field.

Dad was the best person to sit next to at a ballgame. Seems he knew all the players on a first name basis—how, I don't know—and he'd chat 'em up during the game. He even knew about their private lives: "Hey, Gino, I saw your girlfriend, no wonder your ass is draggin' today. Holy Mother of Mercy I got tired just looking at her," and then he'd lean back and roar with laughter.

I had no idea what my dad was yelling out half the time—how can you get tired just looking at a woman—but he'd yell it out with such fervor you had to laugh.

I wish I could hear that laugh again.

As Dad grew older his heart began to fail. I remember one hospital visit when he alternately laughed and cried like a child. "The aftereffects of anesthesia can induce extremes in behavior," the doctor said.

Induce extremes? I knew better. The cigarettes, late nights, and all of his "extremes" were taking their toll.

I listened to his lacerated murmurings. Soon he was able to lift his worn body from the bed. I stared at the curvature of his spine, his hunkered shoulders. I was reminded of the words Joyce used in *The Dead* to describe Gabriel's collision with immortality as my father faded into a "gray impalpable world."

"The goddamned butts caused the problems," Dad said.

Yeah, sure, I thought. What the hell did God have to do with this?

Soon it was time to leave. I walked over to his bed and touched his arm. We just smiled through our tears and shook our heads at each other, gestures that said what we couldn't. This wasn't baseball.

I think my father's garden was his sanctum, a place he would go to find peace. That's where my mother found him. His wool cap had slipped from his head; his shovel lay mute by his side. I'm comforted by that memory. Somehow it seems right.

I think of him often.

I think of him in his garden, digging, a wisp of cigarette smoke curling into his squinting eyes, trying to make sense of the tangle of shadows he'd wrestled with, over and over.

I think of him in the summer . . . with the crack of a bat . . . and in the evening . . . when memories are coaxed by twilight's lengthening shadows.

In the garden, in the summer, and in the evening . . . that's when I think of him.

JULIE EVANS

Julie Evans is a massage therapist, mentor, healer, and writer. A contributing writer and columnist for *Healthy You* magazine, Julie can transform pain and loss into a launching pad for wellness—on the page, on a walk through the woods, and on the massage table. Other publications include *Pulse Magazine* and *Fictionique*. Julie's 2016 memoir, *Joy Road*, documents her story of rejection, addiction, and redemption. Her current writing project collects recipes for hope and healing and is entitled *Visits with Vera*.

STARSTRUCK

Julie Evans

John Denver's "Leaving On A Jet Plane" was my song. I'd sung it dozens of times as I rode my horse, Omar, to see my dad at his warehouse in Rochester, Minnesota, sweat pouring down the sides of his face, his beaming smile as soon as he saw us cantering along the side of the road, me belting out "Babe, I hate to go."

That summer I was ten years old and I had been in the golf club pool for hours, refining my diving and underwater swimming skills. With puckered skin, I slipped on shorts and a top and went off in search of my father. I took a shortcut through the clubhouse down the stairs and out the back door, which overlooked the third hole. Through the tall pine trees that framed the fairway I saw my daddy, seated between a few other club members, at a long folding table near the 18th green. Then I spotted John Denver in mid-swing. John Denver! I'd have recognized him from a mile away.

I watched him smack that ball, saw it toe off the end of his club and soar toward the eighteenth green where it stopped suddenly with a thud, hitting my father hard in the middle of the his forehead.

He fell backward, taking the chair with him. I raced toward him, pushing past the dazed men on either side and put my hands on his cheeks. He was out, and his forehead was already swelling. I looked up and saw John Denver striding quickly toward us. I also saw a single ice cube resting on the grass next to an empty glass that must have been my father's scotch and water. I placed the ice cube on the growing, golf ball size knob on his head and held it there.

"Is that your Daddy?" Mr. Denver asked. "How is he?" I couldn't answer. I was star struck. I had lost track of the ice cube and now all I saw was the famous man's big face and wire-rim glasses.

There was no need to call for a doctor, we were on a golf course in Rochester, Minnesota, surrounded by doctors who all worked for the famous Mayo Clinic. A team of golfer doctors moved me aside as an ambulance pulled up on the grass to take my dad away.

When I got to the hospital, my father was sitting up in bed with two black eyes, his head wrapped with white gauze. And two hours later the famous singer's big face reappeared in the doorway. "I'm fine," he told Mr. Denver. "It's no big deal; I hardly felt it."

John Denver smiled in relief. Dad smiled his most gracious smile. I felt queasy, though, tongue-tied in the presence of the famous man and not so sure everything was fine. I wanted to hit the rock star for hurting my daddy. I also wanted his autograph. And before he left, I wanted him to put his arm around my shoulder and sing, "So kiss me and smile for me, tell me that you'll wait for me, hold me like you'll never let me go."

Seven years later, just four months after my mother died, my father collapsed and a neighbor found him lying in the driveway. The doctors had no clue what had happened, but tests revealed a brain aneurysm behind the exact center of his frontal bone. Right where the golf ball hit him.

The surgeon drilled a hole in the center of my father's forehead and clamped the aneurysm. He was saved. But he was not fine. He was in a coma.

Three weeks later, on the morning of my seventeenth birthday, I put on my prettiest dress and went to St Mary's Hospital and found his empty bed in the Neuro-Intensive Care Unit. I panicked at first, but a nurse took my arm and led me down a corridor to another room where I was sure they were going to sit me down and tell me he was dead, but instead Dad was sitting at a table wearing a white turban of gauze. Before him sat a birthday cake with lit candles and a bouquet of yellow roses. He barely mouthed the words to Happy Birthday.

I was tongue-tied once more.

But as I drove away from the hospital that afternoon, I found my voice, whispering the line, "Already I'm so lonesome I could die."

STEVEN LEWIS

Steven Lewis Literary Ombudsman for 650, is a columnist at *Talking Writing*, and a member of the Sarah Lawrence College Writing Institute faculty. A longtime freelancer, his work has been featured in the *New York Times*, the *Washington Post, Christian Science Monitor*, the *Los Angeles Times, Ploughshares, Spirituality & Health*, and other publications. His novels include *Take This* and *Loving Violet*, both from Codhill Press. Finishing Line Press published Steve's poetry chapbook, *If I Die Before You Wake*. His backlist includes *Zen and the Art of Fatherhood, The ABCs of Real Family Values, The Complete Guide for the Anxious Groom*, and *Fear and Loathing of Boca Raton (a Hippie's Guide to the New Sixties)*. He divides his time between his writing space in New Paltz, New York and Hatteras Island, North Carolina.

NOT MY FATHER'S CADILLAC

Steven Lewis

My father was born in Brooklyn in 1908 and, like so many kids from those immigrant streets, pushed, bulled, and bullied his way through the rough crowds and, as they said back then, made something of himself.

The making did not come without cost, though. In the rubble of the Depression he gave up his dream of practicing law; and down that economic highway he came to an elemental fork: Go left and be a model dad like Ward Cleaver; go right, build a business, and leave the raising of kids to his wife. So, six days a week my father left the house before everyone was awake and twelve hours later came home long after the family had eaten and disappeared behind bedroom doors. Sundays he did paperwork. The man was so industrious, so single-minded, that he missed out on every soccer, baseball, and basketball game I played at Wheatley High. Never went to Ebbets Field. Never took me fishing.

That said, the great sacrifices my old man made did not come without some reward. Applying shoulder to wheel, he made a small business big enough to buy a ranch house on suburban Candy Lane

29

(yes, Candy Lane). And a few years later traded the dependable Buick for his dreamboat, a 1956 Cadillac Coupe de Ville.

My old man stood next to that powder blue beauty with a driveway-wide grin. His brothers, Murray (Hawaiian shirts) and Mac (argyle kneesocks), who also made somethings of themselves, drove Chrysler Imperials. There was no contest.

I was pleased as punch for my dad, at least until I began to wonder if it was possible he liked the Caddy more than me. And during the reign of the second Coupe de Ville, the '59 with the big gaudy fins, I finally bellowed out all my adolescent confusion and frustration, pointing right at the behemoth in the garage.

He had no idea what I was ranting about.

So in 1968, when Patti got pregnant and Dad was just settling into Cadillac number five, I righteously vowed never to put money or career before family. . . I would be a good dad. A great dad. If God Himself had pulled an Abraham on me, I would gladly submit to plague, pestilence, and Plymouths before I sacrificed my child . . . or owned a Cadillac.

So, you know where this is going . . . but let me drive you there my own route. I went on to lead the life I threatened I would. Went to every game, every concert, every ceremony, standing proudly next to my seven kids just as he stood beaming beside his Cadillacs. And from the driver's seat of a long succession of VW Vans and other clunky counter-culture cars full of stickers and dents and the spills of seven children, I found myself driving a rusty Honda Passport that whined and grunted and practically begged me to put it down.

Which was when, as these things happen in the karmic circle of life, my wife got a call from her father who had recently bought a Cadillac SRX and hated driving it. He offered it to us. For free!

Thus caught in the one-way traffic jam of my own making, I bellowed, "No! Look at me. I'm a beach dog! I'm a hipster! I have a f---ing ponytail!"

She looked at me like I was nuts. Like my late father would have looked at me.

She was right, of course.

So there I was all those incarnations later, Samuel Lewis' angry boy, all grown up and commandeering that Capitalist Pigmobile down Main Street in our funky upstate town, enduring endless razzing from friends and foes—and, what's worse, enjoying driving that lavish beast.

And for the first time gaining an appreciation for my father's pleasures . . . and the cosmic-sized sacrifices that went into attaining them.

Eventually the novelty faded, though, and I traded down for something I could drive on a beach. But when I handed over the keys to the salivating Toyota salesman, I realized that while my father may not have been a model dad like Ward Cleaver, as a son I was one big, ungrateful pain in the ass.

EDWARD McCANN

Edward McCann is an award winning writer/producer and the founder and editor of **650**, a literary forum that celebrates the spoken word with live events in New York City and elsewhere. A longtime contributing editor to *Country Living*, his features and essays have been published in many literary journals, anthologies, and national magazines, including *Milieu, Better Homes & Gardens, Good Housekeeping, The Irish Echo, The Sun,* and others. His essay, "Pregnant Again," was selected for the anthology, *Listen To Your Mother,* published by Penguin, and he's recently completed a memoir about the search for his missing nephew. A member of New York City-based Artists Without Walls, he lives and writes in New York's Hudson River Valley.

THE APOLOGY
Edward McCann

I am the son of a man who was quick with his hands and slow to offer any praise; a man who quit drinking years before my birth, but who hadn't quit being angry.

I was twelve and my brother Jim was fourteen in 1975—the last two of six children still at home when my parents sold our house in Queens and moved us to a retirement community in sunny central Florida. I looked at our new home—a pastel, cinderblock and stucco house next door to Mom's elderly Aunt Millie and Uncle Harold with no idea what our future held.

In December, just a few months after we arrived, Uncle Joe's wife, Anne, died in Brooklyn. Millie and Harold needed to get to New York immediately, but a freak snowstorm had closed JFK—or Idlewild, as my father continued to call it long after the name had been changed. Dad offered to drive Millie and Harold the thousand miles home to Brooklyn for their sister-in-law's wake and funeral, so they packed right away and drove through the night.

A week later, my father returned to Florida, to his home surrounded by grapefruit trees and sago palms, no longer looking so angry. The scowl etched into his face from years of furrowed concentration on pipe fittings and technical manuals and crossword puzzles was gone. He sat in his chair at the dining table, sipping an amber drink over ice and telling my mother about the trip, about the great piles of snow, and about watching Uncle Joe photograph his wife's body in the casket.

At twelve I didn't grasp the significance of the alcohol on the table and didn't know it was the first time in decades he'd had anything to drink at all. The remarkable thing was that it was the first time I ever saw my father cry.

Mom busied herself at the sink and Dad set his glass down, dried his eyes with the backs of his balled fists, and beckoned my brother Jimmy and me toward him. He gathered us in his arms and held us close, something he'd never done before. "I know I haven't always been a good father to you boys," Dad said as fresh tears flowed down his face, "and I'm sorry." His voice broke, and in a strangled sob he added, "I shouldn't have even had you kids; I was too old to be the kind of father you needed."

My older brother and sisters had a father who drank, a man who sometimes sang and played piano or played the spoons against his thigh. That wasn't the man who raised me; I'd gotten a dry drunk with an explosive temper whom I'd never seen touch a piano or a drink. Yet that day, with our arms crossed and tangled around him, Jimmy and I held our father as he wept and trembled; we told him that we loved him, that we wouldn't trade him for any other dad in the world.

The funeral—and then the alcohol Dad sipped—had unlocked something deep inside him, revealing a dimension of the man I'd never seen before. The drink on the table before him was a dose of truth serum, a magic potion; and like the WD-40 in his old tool kit, it had somehow lubricated and loosened a part of him that had long ago seized and rusted.

Even as his health was failing from asbestos exposure and decades of smoking—things that also pre-dated my birth—I noticed that my new, more relaxed and congenial father seemed to tell more jokes, and was enjoying—finally, in his brief retirement—the occasional highball or Tom Collins or beer he'd denied himself for years.

Three years later, at fifteen, I was the last one in the viewing chapel the morning of my father's burial. I placed my palms flat on his chest, cold and unyielding as a block of marble beneath layers of wool and cotton, then rested my warm hands over my father's cold ones. I spoke with him then, telling him things I'd never told anyone and asking questions that can never be answered.

Thirty-six years later, I've moved far away from the pastel world of that Florida retirement community. I don't know what my father would think of the life I'm living today with Richard Kollath in upstate New York, but I feel his presence in a few quiet corners of our house—in the secretary desk where he once sat to write his bills, in his depression era, paint-encrusted aluminum stepladder, and in a bucket of his old wrenches I keep in the shed. And I feel him still in the memory of that single apology for the man he wasn't, and the father he wished he'd been.

MALACHY MCCOURT

Malachy McCourt was born in Brooklyn, New York, and from the age of three was raised in Limerick, Ireland. He returned to New York at age twenty, working manual jobs until he became an actor, with roles on Broadway, off-Broadway, on television, and in film. Malachy's writing been published in *New York Newsday*, *National Geographic*, *Conscience Magazine* and *The New York Times*. With his brother, Frank, he co-authored the play *A Couple of Blaguards* and has written his own New York Times bestselling memoir, *A Monk Swimming*. His most recent book is *Death Need Not Be Fatal*. Other books include *Singing My Him Song*, *Danny Boy*, *The Claddagh Ring*, *Voices of Ireland*, and *Malachy McCourt's History of Ireland*. Happily married to Diana for more than four decades, Malachy has five grown children, is grandfather to four, and owes a great deal to his friend, Bill W.

36

A MONK SWIMMING
Malachy McCourt

The day, the early summer day, when he took me by the hand to go for the walk, I was eager, because he rarely held our hand or carried anything in his own, as he believed it was unseemly for a man to care for a child or to carry a parcel in his hands. "Woman's work," sez he!

We walked out by the way of Rosbrien, past the White Gates of the Railway, past the small houses the English built for railway workers. He told me we were going to a place where there is a well that has the sweetest, coolest magical spring waters, which are there to make you happy. I just couldn't get over how much I loved my daddy then, for bringing me to this sacred, secret place. We clambered over one stile, and crossed a field that had cows who looked at me and frightened me, but big, brave father chased them off with a wave of his hand. Over a ditch we went with him, me carried above the clumps of stinging nettles, which he said were good for you when brewed as tea.

We walked to the middle of the field, and there, midst a clump of rushes, was the well. It didn't look to me like it was too magical, as it was just water, surrounded by some built-up stones. "Kneel down and drink it," he said, and I did. I tried to remember something I'd read in a Bible about soldiers being selected for battle by Moses, and whether they cupped their hands and drank the water, or was it that they put their mouths in the water and sucked it up?

I thought it was braver to put my mouth in the water and suck it up. It was the loveliest water I'd ever tasted, and the more I drank of it, the lovelier it became. And then we lay under a big shady tree, which was the home of dozens of birds, and my father made up stories of bravery and dying for Ireland, and he sang many songs, and recited poetry, and manufactured tales of the doings of the shapes in the clouds. The bees hummed, the birds sang, and the insects cricketed all around us as he talked, crooned, and made great use of the language to fill a child's mind with joy and wonder.

The marvelous sun began its descent in the sky, and all around us the natives of nature began the rustling and settling for the evening's rest. My dad told me that all creatures had one thing in common: They all knew how to pray. That's what they were doing now—thanking God for another blessed and wonderful day, and we should go now and leave them to their devotions.

The darkness was falling as we walked back along the road to the fetid lane, and there were scary moos and caws, and screeches from the fields on either side of us, but my dad picked me up and held me close, and I wasn't afraid anymore, and I fell asleep and didn't wake 'til the next morning.

When my father left us and went to England, I went to find the well again. Over the same stile I went, over the same ditch, where the stinging nettles threatened, past the big sheltering tree, to where the well had been. It wasn't there: no rushes, no well.

I tramped all over that field, and the field to the south of it, and to the north of it, and every other field, but never again did I find that well, and ever again did I find the father who brought me there.

ACKNOWLEDGMENTS

In addition to the contributors to this volume, we thank **Nancy Manocherian's** *the cell*, which supported 650 at its inception. A twenty-first century salon in the heart of New York City, their mission is to support the arts and to incubate new works, and the cell made its beautiful performance space available to 650 as we were finding our way. The cell: To mine the mind, pierce the heart, and awaken the soul.
TheCellTheatre.org

Artists Without Walls was created to inspire, uplift and unite people and communities of diverse cultures through the pursuit of artistic achievement, and has supported and encouraged 650 from its beginnings. Artists Without Walls: No Limits. No Walls. No Boundaries.
ArtistsWithoutWalls.com

We thank **The New Rochelle Public Library** for its generous support of 650, and for stimulating and encouraging the study and presentation of the performing and fine arts. Throughout the year, NRCA sponsors many exhibitions, theatrical productions, dance recitals, film screenings, lectures, and concert series.
NRPL.org

www.ingramcontent.com/pod-product-compliance
Lightning Source LLC
Chambersburg PA
CBHW072046170626
46811CB00008B/3180